for my children

Contents

PREFACE   ix

OPENING ONESELF

Freedom Swagger   3
The Roar   4
Face Peeling   8
Emptying   11
Perhaps   13
Wound Fondling   16
Faith   18
Woman Alive   19
Solitude   22
Transition   24

OPENING TO OTHERS

Wedding Poem   29
Friend   30
Grace   32
The Landing   34
Fearlessly Alive   38
Opening Again   41
Down   44
Wounding Game   46
Coupling   48
My Lovers   51

Opening To Greater Forces

Ritual	55
Destiny Arrives	56
Shift	60
Baptism	63
Unwanted	65
Mother	67
Death of a Hero	70
And She Rises	73
Broken Glass	74

Preface

For the past fifteen years I have carried around in my pocket, my purse or my notebook an untitled poem by Ranier Maria Rilke with the following three lines highlighted:

> *I want to unfold.*
> *I don't want to be folded anywhere.*
> *Because where I am folded there I am a lie.*

Rilke's words have been my constant companion because they are a reminder of my own deep desire to open completely. They also illuminate the intimate relationship between opening and truth. *Opening Again* is an exploration of continued opening and the transformations that result. For those of you engaged in transformational healing work, I hope this book will be an inspiration and a comfort.

Each of the poems started as an image, a dream, a curious encounter or a feeling that would not go away. They were birthed on a subconscious level, but as I wrote them down and shaped them I realized they were a way to ground my own learning.

The word parable is included in the subtitle because a number of the poems have been used by groups and individuals as teaching, healing tools. If you choose to use *Opening Again* in this way, please read the poems that call to you slowly and aloud. Notice if you sense an opening, however subtle, anywhere in your body; it may be as simple as a smile or a sigh.

The poems, with the exception of *Wedding Poem,* were written in the past two years. I am well into my forties now, and so there is an element of midlife passage represented here. Also apparent in these pages is my love affair with the feminine divine. She speaks to me primarily through my body, my intuition, my connection to the earth; and it is this energy that fuels my writing.

So as a woman unfolding, embracing the feminine, I am feeling, as written in *Freedom Swagger:*

Finally
And once again
Free

It is from this place of freedom and trust that I wish you well in your unfolding. It is also from this place that I have the courage and imagination to envision a cultural maturation and transformation — an exquisite collective opening in which we may be already unknowingly immersed.

Opening Oneself

Freedom Swagger

I step into the early morning light
There is a swing in my hips
My chin floats a little higher
My shoulders roll with every step
With delight I recognize my movement
I have begun to swagger
I am walking down the road
Doing the Freedom Swagger

Today I am an entitled child
The world in this moment
Has been made for me
Hazy sunlight feeds my eyes
Newly ripe raspberries leap into my mouth
Gnats and dewdrops tease my legs and ankles
And the singing redbird
Sitting in the bush to my left
Flies straight into my heart

And I swagger on
The summer swagger of childhood
Finally
And once again
Free

○

The Roar

He lies next to his wife
A woman he half loves
In a hotel room near an airport
It could be any hotel near any airport
He could be any man
Who loves with half his heart
Who shuffles like a shadow
Who speaks in half truths
And lives a life
That happened to him

Sometime after midnight
A mistaken stranger
With his room numbers confused
Rattles the door handle of the man's room
And attempts to insert a key
Perhaps it is the intensity of the fear
In his half sleeping state that opens the gate
Perhaps it is grace
But the man in the bed begins to roar

It is a huge and chilling roar
The man is shocked at himself
But he cannot stop it
The roar has entered his body
Through his pelvic floor
It lifts him out of the bed
Onto his feet
Twists him slightly
Flings back his head
Stretches open his jaw
Grabs hold of his tongue

It is a wild deep animal sound
The air around him quickens
And becomes red hot
The room begins to quiver
The stranger is frightened off
The woman is terrified
And the roar continues

The sound that had lifted him up
Now takes him down
He has to crawl on his belly
Through the vibrating tunnel of this roar
That is ripping open his chest
He didn't create the roar
But it is moving through him now
And somewhere in the midst
Of this ancient pulsating sound
Emanating from his mouth
He commits to it
He lets the roar define him

When it is finished
The man and the woman
Lie back on the bed
Silent and stunned
Finally he laughs
Then she laughs
A laughter that leaps and guffaws
A free laughter
A loud laughter
Laughter they have never shared
They laugh themselves breathless

When he returns home from the airport
The next afternoon
It is gray and drizzling
He takes off his shoes
And walks barefoot into the garden
His feet sink into the damp earth
He crouches down
And digs his hands into the mud as well

Inside, his body is still vibrating
From the sound of the roar
His throat opens again
This time the sound is softer
A slow deep solid moan
The moan of a man
Who has just given birth to himself

O

Face Peeling

This past spring and summer
I have been engaged in a process
Of peeling off my skin
Specifically the skin of my face
Not a rebirthing, a revealing

Unbeknownst to me
When I agreed to be visible
I made a covenant of sorts
With invisible forces

I unknowingly called
A circle of souls
Not all of them pleasant
Whose purpose in gathering
Has been to assist me
In peeling away my skin
Not a shedding, a stripping

Not as painful
As I thought
Quicker than imagined
Awkward and disconcerting
I have avoided mirrors

Then yesterday at a luncheon
A woman about my age
With thick glasses and sharp eyes
Whispered to me on the stairs

I like your face
It's scary
She examined me again
Nice, but scary
And she was gone

And so it is done
My circle has dispersed
I have been revealed
It is so lovely
To be seen

Yes, my new face is edgy
The bones are closer to the surface
My skin, however
Is folded with kindness
My eyes are vast

Having braved reflection
I like my new face
It is malleable and alive
It divulges my past
Shouts my destiny
It attracts fellow faces
Willing to be known

○

Emptying

She sits cross-legged
On a rough wooden floor
Her hands move deliberately
She is laying out her sins

Having taken
Her weapons, her crutches
Out of the bushes
She is emptying her pockets
Ripping out the lining
Splaying open her dark deeds

Having dusted away
The shame forced upon her
The guilt that is hers
She claims

She gathers up
The distorted fragments
Builds a visible altar
Allowing others to see

Having released her vision
Of mythical angels
Methodically dismantled
All hope of redemption
She knows now
She can choose to be open
She will never be clean

○

Perhaps

He should have been suckled on truth
Instead he was fed a joy obsession
Schooled in the pursuit of joy
Groomed in the appearance of it

This lust for joy led to the sky
His initial flights were lovely
He had a talent for flying
Lifting, gliding, spiraling
A weightless wonder in the air

But his early training held
He had no stomach for the coming down
Driven inside to go higher, faster
In a sky so grand
He craved it all

Landings became progressively rougher
He turned away from those
Meant to teach him
He preferred an isolated thrill

Eventually, he crashed
Annoyed by his compulsive presence
The sky dropped him
Tossed him down on the rocks
As a seagull smashes a shell

For many days
He has lain on the beach
Barely breathing
Completely still

Perhaps it's done

Or perhaps
He is quietly being healed
By this dark, delicious
Human, imperfect world
He tried to rise above

Perhaps it's done

Or perhaps he will fly again
Joy will surprise him
Joy will lift him up
The sky will stretch him open

Then he will choose
A grace-filled, grateful landing
On this living, honest
Gray-green earth
He will have learned to love

○

Wound Fondling

Be wary of the wound fondlers
They will attempt to engage you
In an obscene ritual
That may leave you
Weak, exposed or nearly dead

If you suspect a wound fondler
Notice the hands
Look for long slender fingers
Pale in nature
Suspiciously soft
Fingers that never stop moving

Wound fondlers
Won't meet your gaze
Their eyes so straight to your scars
They will listen kindly
To your story of hurt and betrayal
This is a seduction

What they want
Is to dig their fingers
Into your wound
They want to enter you
Stimulate your pain

They will slyly suggest
That you relive your wounding
After hours of probing
They will reopen the incision
Wider, deeper

Wound fondlers
Know the language
They have been wounded, too
Remember your wounds
Belong only
To you

○

Faith

For a time
She had to step back from religion
A difficult movement

For a time
She had to sever all visible chords
Relinquish her savior

For a time
She had to release her beliefs
Abide in her senses

She had to stumble
Through the darkness
Find the deepest part of her
And feel her faith

○

Woman Alive

One spring day
Early in the morning
In the middle of her life
She knew it was time

She opened the front door
With a great deal of fear
A lifetime ago
She had been stoned
And then burned
For the very thing
She was about to do

She stepped out on her front porch
With no clothing or covering of any kind
Sat down on the cool stones
And opened her legs
Revealing the center point
Of earthly pleasure
And the power source of all new birth

As she warmed herself
In the rising sun
Her throat opened as well
And the tone she sounded
Was deep, dark, ancient
And true

People began to pass by
Many never noticed her
Nor could they hear her voice
Their eyes were focused
On their own roads

Others shouted at her
Shaming, degrading, accusing
Threatening to destroy
But she kept her rage in front of her
Her grief alive inside her
And none of them came near

Others were called — drawn to her
They heard her sound from across town
When they saw her sitting there
So open and so brave
They smiled so deeply
Their faces were changed forever

At the end of the day
She was still alive
She stood then in the moonlight
Tears streaming from her eyes
Moistening, strengthening
Her breasts, her belly, her feet

Stronger now
And safe enough
She opened her arms
Her heart wide
She became
A living, breathing prayer

○

Solitude

There are moments
Long, timeless moments
When solitude becomes
My deepest adventure
Alone
I enter myself
Like a lover

I abandon definition
Feast on dreams and visions
Welcome the soft, gray
Mystery of death
I feel my breath
As though for the first time
Perhaps the last

These are the moments
Of my greatest opening
I open like a vowel
Like a hand
Like the toothless yawn
Of a sleepy infant

I open like the arms of a mother
Reunited with her lost child
Open like a yellow daffodil
Unleashed by spring
I open like the face
Of one who has just engaged
In a surprisingly true
Wholly unexpected
Kiss

○

Transition

I'm standing in ashes
Searching the sky for smoke
It's time to move on
I'm looking for the next fire

For me it has always been fire
Flames that have called to me
Burned me, moved me
Dragged me from my inert slumbers

Fires of passion, creative fire
Fires that have destroyed
Fires that have transformed
Fires I have had to put out

Older now and worn
I stand here in the ashes
Of all my many tended fires
I see new growth, strong roots, decay
All with a life of its own
I am finished here

As I raise my tired eyes to the horizon
Searching again the sky for smoke
Quite unexpectedly
I smell the sea
The ageless, cleansing
Limitless, forgiving
Folding and unfolding sea

○

*Opening
To
Others*

Wedding Poem

We meet in the in-between place
The space between moments

When daylight rests
And rich full night begins

Where separations soften
Where separations end

Here spirits sweat when they make love
Bodies move in prayer

With warm soft animal bellies
With clear angelic hearts

We answer yes to life
Yes to one another
Yes to the world

We birth our union into form

○

Friend

You are water and earth
I am fire and air
You are voluptuous, full-bodied, deeply rooted
You speak in whispers of deep sensuality
Of the power of the river of life
Of the ancient secrets of women
You are a blessing

I am slender and strong
In love with solitary flight
My fire, my passion
Is for clean air, freedom, clarity
And upward spirals of truth

When I crash
When I am scorched and shaking
From too much internal fire
Too much earthly burden
You cool me, comfort me, honor me
And I am healed

If ever your waters grow stagnant
Your roots become heavy
You find yourself
Abandoned and alone
I will lift you up
I will lend you my wings

○

Grace

Sitting in the shade
A few yards from the pool
I watch with fascination
The strong, long tanned legs
Of my newly adolescent daughter
She is climbing the ladder
To the high diving board

With a cool sadness
I realize
That for the first time
In her life
I am seeing her
From a distance

As she steps onto the board
In a striped orange bikini
She bought to match her older cousin's
I know she thinks
The whole world is watching her

She is correct
The whole world is watching her
Because she is beautiful
And because we humans
Are visually riveted
To those who stand between worlds
As she does now

As she perches
On the tip of that quivering board
I exhale release
And blush quiet embarrassment
With the thought
That this almost woman
Ever belonged to me
Then I say a prayer
For my once child

My prayer for Grace
Is the image I have of her
Swimming strongly
Cavorting freely
Fluidly faithful
Dolphin-like
In the deep pool
Of her adult self

○

The Landing

Stiff with apprehension
I watch from the bedroom window
As my young son
Races down the driveway
On rollerblades
Twists around obstacles
Mounts a makeshift ramp
He has devised
Hurls himself into the air
Attempts a complete circle
And a landing
On moving wheels

He fails
He examines the hip
On which he fell
The knee he scraped
Is slightly bleeding
Convinced he is still intact
He whizzes back up the driveway
To repeat this rolling ritual
With greater velocity

This is the child
I birthed into a cloud of fear
Wounded on his first day
I clutched him tightly
Crouching in corners
Frightened by hospitals, needles
And authoritative voices

His body healed
But he inherited the fear
At times it fogs his mind
Fills his dreams

Silently I watch him
Riding the waves of fear
There on the pavement
Twisting and flipping
Risking himself again and again
Opening to possibilities
Of freedom and of flight

Finally with one momentous leap
He executes the perfect 360
Lands smoothly
High fives the air

Then my son turns
Looks directly at the window
Where I am standing
He is in bright sunlight
I am in shadow
Still his eyes
Seem to find me

With a grin, a jump
An overhead flick of his wrist
As though shooting a basket
He tosses back
All the anxiety
I christened him with years ago
Tosses it back to me
Like an old rubber ball
He doesn't want to play with any longer

Astonished, I catch it
It belongs to me
Embarrassed at being seen
I begin to chuckle
Begrudgingly at first
Then with delight

I watch one moment longer
He skates back up the hill
Focused on repeating
The perfect 360
Focused on creating
His own unencumbered life

○

Fearlessly Alive

A weekend ritual
Parents stepping out of vans
Loaded with water bottles, snacks
Canvas folding chairs

Children are already
On the field
Neon bright jerseys
Matching socks

Cassandra is easy to spot
A pony tailed blonde
The only girl
In a field sprouting boys

Oblivious to me
She is in an altered state
Focused only on the game
Her sacred ceremony of choice
Youth Soccer

She is my youngest
The child I did not choose
The one who chose me
Since her conception
I have followed her lead

Whistle blows
She moves sideways
Across the earth
Conscious of position
Viscerally aware

Leaning slightly forward
Breathing through her nostrils
Eyes in constant motion
Tenacious, unswerving
She blocks one shot
And then another

I want to step onto the field
Politely excuse myself
And my daughter
Wrap her in my gray hooded sweatshirt
Hide her light
Keep her safe

This girl knows power
Power born of pleasure
Married to motion
When I rub her back at night
Her muscles sing

The ball is hers
She pulls away
Dribbles down the field
Maneuvers with grace
Passes swiftly to a teammate
He scores

Now grinning broadly
Her face horizontal with joy
Both arms in the air
She breaks into beauty
Celebrates her team
We cheer

I am her mother
I brush her hair
Fold her clothes
Feed her well
She follows my rules

But in the practice
Of being fearlessly alive
Cassandra is my mentor
My guide

○

Opening Again

She is considering the possibility
Of making love to a man
Who betrayed her again and again

This is how he betrayed her
He gathered his huge, blind, heavy will
And wrapped her in it tightly
Like a cloak without buttons

She lived so long
Inside this garment of his making
That when she looked down at her body
She could no longer see her flesh
Only the rough brown fabric of his will
That covered her
That colored her

Once she was contained
He carelessly hurled
Stones of responsibility in her direction
She had to contort herself
Distort herself
To catch those stones
But she did
She knew no other way

As children grew up around her
Planting themselves in her heart
Entwining themselves in her legs
She could no longer move her feet
Fearing she would fly away
He stripped her wings of feathers
All the while asking her
To be his muse

He could not however
Drown her rage
Every act of betrayal
Fueled it
Until iron-jawed, sharp-eyed
Red hot rage was her identity
Until her body was no longer
Discolored by his will
But rather glowing with a rage
That belonged to her

Then she betrayed him
Or so it seemed
She stopped opening to him
No more opening at all
When he was near

Instead she opened inward
And in those days and years
Of inner openings
She became familiar
With the feel of freedom

She told herself the truth
She built her own altar
She aroused herself
She learned about receiving
From friends, from water, from trees
She dressed lightly
In sheer clothing of amber and rose
She played in her dreams

Now she is wanting
To open to him again
Not from obligation or forgiveness
Or even hopefulness
But because finally inner openings
Must become outer ones
Because the possibility
Of making love to him anew
Makes her feel freer still

And so she will
With her eyes open
And her wings intact

○

Down

I need to go way down
Under the water
Immerse myself in fluids
Where I breathe with my cells
Instead of my lungs
Where grunts and moans
Are my only language
I need to go way down
To make love to you

Still I hold myself up
Above the surface
With my own charged-up
Lifted-up
Wound-up mind
My tribe and I
We choose to live
With our heads
In a time vise
It's tight
It hurts

So lover
Lead me down
Down to where you swell and harden
Down to where I soften and open
I need a respite, a retreat
A horizontal hiatus
From this sharp and scary
Rapid train of thinking
Lead me down
Let me flower

○

Wounding Game

What have I done?
I have always been sharp
Handled knives
With great success and care
Why did I cut you this time?

I meant to prick you just a bit
To draw a feeling, a movement, a change
I used the same blade
Same pressure, same timing
Same placement I always have

But you turned slightly
And the knife slipped in
Slipped in so deeply
I lost my balance
The blade went deeper still

Your eyes are frozen
Startled by pain
My body stiff with shame
My careless cruelty
Chills the room

I am standing here
With my hand in your chest
Stuck in your wound
Sealed together
In an ancient wounding game
Perhaps forever

What will we do?
I hold the knife
But I must ask you
To let me go

○

Coupling

Moved by passion, propriety
And a strange inner desire
They stepped into marriage
Their hearts stumbled after

Marriage initially
Formed a medieval container
They donned suits of armor
Began a confined clanging march
Welded together
In rigid predictable expression

Enraged with patterned living
They stretched their marriage
To the point of almost breaking
Risking enlarged their union
Space for laughter
Room to dance

As they continued to couple
A wrestling match ensued
Bodies entangled sweating
Pushing against each other
Matching their wills
Muscle to muscle
Afraid of winning and losing

Exhausted from hiding their pain
They finally surrendered
Revealed themselves
To one another
Learned to struggle honestly
And refuse all weapons

As they weathered
Their marriage became
A house of mirrors
The distorted demons
They spied in the hallways
Frightened them into withdrawal
As did sin and betrayals
They believed belonged to the other

Guidance and stillness
Cleared their vision
They claimed their shadows
All the dark and all the light
In both of them
They had to swallow
It nourished them
They grew whole enough
To hold each other

Having truly committed
Having felt themselves
And the other so deeply
They prepare themselves now
For the end of this life
And the loss of the other

May the blessing of their gift
The enormity of their grief
Soften them completely
Dissolve all separation
May their final hours be infused
With an enduring gratitude
A gratitude that says
Because of you
I am

○

My Lovers

I'm a middle-aged woman
Partnered and true
Who will not limit her loving
In fact, I refuse

There are men and women
I have known and will know
Who arouse me and please me
And help me unfold

I hold these sweet souls
Not as mother or healer
We are sensual beings
Creating together

There's strength to this loving
It's a kind of an art
No obsession, possession
Just a wide open heart

Whole body choices
These precious encounters
I am infinitely grateful
For all of my lovers

○

*Opening
To
Greater
Forces*

Ritual

Deeper into the circle
Until I am the circle
A circle within circles
Spherically divine

Swinging backward
Swinging forward
Time folding inward
My separate self
Sliding away

Infused with Goddess
Drenched in God
Ecstasy summons me
Beauty releases me

Engorged with movement
Shot through with sensation
Shattering, splintering
Into so many prisms

Shimmering, shaken
And reawakened
Engulfed in belonging
I return home

○

Destiny Arrives

Circumstances
Opinions of others
Moments of grace
Have shaped my life
Having had no known encounters
With Destiny
I was surprised last winter
When she began to reveal herself
In my dreams

This morning I opened the door
To find Destiny
Romping with the dog
In the front yard
Dressed in burnt sienna
And a vivid shade of aquamarine
She was snarling playfully
With the family beast

In what felt like
The grandest gesture of my life
I invited her in for tea

She refused the porcelain teacup
I offered her
Requested instead
The misshapen mug
My niece had created in preschool
She held it in her thick calloused hands
Added milk and honey

She told me stories about myself
That were true — or could be
Stories I had forgotten
Each account made me laugh
She laughed too
With her mouth wide open
Even tales of loss and pain
Nourished me

I fell in love with her so quickly
I wanted to consume her
Ingest my destiny
With her robust color
Her deep sparkling voice
Her rich musky flesh

I had grown thin and pale
This morning I was hungry
Ravenously hungry
So I devoured my destiny
Swallowed every bit of her
Without thought or hesitation
Consumed this seductive willing meal
Until finally I was full

Hours have passed
It is evening now
My body is feverish
My mind frenetic
Everything is changing
I can feel it
My voice, my breath
My blood, the world

Others who are visited
Pit their wills against their destinies
Or wait for another
They negotiate, compromise
Not I, I gave into lust
A lust for more life
I relinquished my will
Instantaneously
Was I brave?
Or was I foolish?

I lay me down to sleep
With no idea
Who I will be
When I awake

○

Shift

He has always been certain
This tall, intelligent man
Who abides in a vertical world
Focused, invincible
Taut and slim
Preferring sharp delineations
And living on pinnacles

Last night there was a shift
A cool autumn evening
Alone in his automobile
He entered the driveway
Of his suburban home
He could not see
The ginger cat
Who scampered across his path
Among the gold and yellow leaves

When his car hit the cat
With a dull thud
He left the car running
As he got out quickly
Bent down to examine
The dead or dying animal
Lying in the leaves
A few yards away

It was a peculiar sight
This perpetually upright man
Squatting in the near darkness

Finally he allowed himself a sigh
A warm, deep, heavy sigh
A sound that frightened him
With that sigh
He felt as though
He were liquid
As though he were melting

His vision blurred
Then widened
He saw himself as fallible
Helpless, mortal
His belly softened
He began to unravel

He then had the strange urge
To let himself be defeated
To lie down on the ground
In the fallen leaves
Next to the broken body
Of the tiny cat
He longed to grieve her death
To grieve his past
To grieve

It was the motor of the car
And the repetitive electronic chime
Signaling that the door was open
That called him back to the familiar
But the shift had occurred
His descent was beginning

He parked his car in the garage
Picked up the cat's body
Placed it in a garbage can
Covered it gently with newspaper
Then went inside
To tell his wife
To tell his daughter
Their kitten had died

○

Baptism

The newborn sleeps
Briefly she fears
While the woman rocks relentlessly
Her once small breasts
Have become extremely large
Boulder hard

She perspires endlessly, profusely
Her milk flows freely
Fluids run down her torso
Drenching her pink gown
And the wide, horizontal bandage
Covering the gash in her belly

She is frightened
Frightened of drowning her child
Suffocating him in sweetness
She is frightened of failing
Frightened of losing her own life

The baby cries
Milk shoots out of her engorged nipples
So much sticky, sweaty milk
It's dripping from the ceiling now
Running down the walls

No circle of women here
To hold her and bless her
No elder, no mentor
But she is baptized, nonetheless
Baptized into motherhood
By her own excreting breasts

○

Unwanted

I know nothing of snakes
Except that I fear them

Mostly I live my life
As though there are no snakes
I organize and function
As though nothing
Cold, soundless and ancient
Exists in my world

But recently my father
Found an empty skin
In the backyard
Two weeks later
There she was
Sunning herself on a low-hanging branch
Near the front porch

I watched her for a long time
I watched her both coiled and relaxed
I watched when she arched and tunneled in the air
I watched her tongue quiver and dance

I was stunned
Unwanted, she had slithered in
Through a crack in my conscious mind

Now the fear of her is with me faithfully
In moments I can barely breathe
I have not seen her in weeks
But, of course, she is still here

In listening for her
I have begun to listen to her
Do I fear her?
Or is she my fear?

I know nothing of snakes
Except that I fear them
And I surrender
To a life that includes them

○

Mother

Every morning
While the others are sleeping
She descends the stairs to the kitchen
She rises only
To prepare the house for them

As she walks down the steps
She chooses an image for the day
An image of herself
As a mother

Today perhaps
She will see herself
As a huge and milky breast
Or a gracious queen
A giving tree
Or a sacrificial lamb
Torn into pieces
And stuffed
Into hungry little mouths

She chooses these images
To shape her life with meaning
These mental visions lift her up
Carry her through the day
Like tiny white balloons
Filled with hope
And the dry dust of doubt
She floats alone

What she does not know
Could not know
Because she has not been gifted
With a guide
Is that below her feet
Beneath her skin
Deep in her belly
Flows an underground river
The living moving archetype
Of Mother

This sacred river
Is a place of communion
For all mothers
There are rapids of rage
Whirlpools of chaotic grief
Waves of intense joy
Pain, engagement
And still pools in which to rest

Here live all the other mothers
Who have gone before
This is the river
That She, the Goddess Herself
Birthed so long ago

If the woman
Could open herself
To this ancient force
She would be stretched, fully dilated
Her children would thrive
Would find their own callings
She would be a woman transfigured
An artist, a visionary, a healer
And nothing else would matter

○

Death of a Hero

The hero is dead
I knew him well

During his celebrated life
He slay an enormous
Mutilating dragon
He breathed life and fire
Into a cold and empty kingdom
He inspired younger heroes
It is good that he lived

Yet life at home
Was hard for the hero
He was never still enough
To be nurtured and receive
Fear and doubt tortured the hero
Trickling continually
Down the back his neck
The length of his spine
He grew rigid and stiff
He rarely slept

It was a surprise encounter
With his past
That finally killed him

He met again
A child he had saved
Who had not needed saving
And a woman he had injured
Permanently damaged
With his righteousness

In the presence
Of an imperfect past
A hero cannot breathe
And so he perished

The man he left behind
The man who was always there
Has eyes so soft
Skin so porous
That he does not separate himself
From ugliness or beauty
Strong in his bones
His heart will stretch

For the man remaining
Life is not only a mission
Life is an expression of trust
An extended moment
A blessing

○

And She Rises

And she rises
She rises up from the earth
Dark, moist and steaming
With grand swaying breasts
And thick full thighs

Her body undulates with pleasure
She smells of dirt and decay
And also of fruit and roses
Her eyes reflect the moon
Her hands are as old as water

Her beauty is too mutable to be seen
Hers is a beauty that must be felt
It spirals up from beneath us
This beauty that includes us

She is rising now
And if we allow it
We will be held
We will be suckled
We will be birthed again and again
By this great and grounding mother

Broken Glass

A shattered wine glass
On the floor
Red wine pooling
On white ceramic tile
Dropped carelessly
The last remnant
Of a first marriage

Staring at the shimmering
Slivers of glass
Running red rivulets
I consider containers
Containers I have broken
With lust and rage
Containers I have created
With commitment and grace

Containers held by others
Healing circles
That have transformed me
Precise containers
Alchemy's tools
The container of time
Cupping my life

Squatting in the kitchen
Picking up shards of glass
I notice my hands
My aging body
The container to which
I am most attached

Kneeling now
I find myself
Mourning my own death
The loss of this body
These hands
And my exquisitely
Beautiful life

O